HEALING
RELATIONSHIPS
THROUGH FORGIVENESS

REQUESTING GOD'S GRACE
FROM OTHERS

A GROUP STUDY
PART 2

DONALD E. JONES, PHD

J & A BOOK PUBLISHERS
www.jabookpublishers.com

ISBN-13: 978-0692740613
ISBN-10: 0692740619

DEDICATION

I dedicate this book to my Savior and Lord Jesus Christ. He has been with me every step of my journey upon the earth, and I so look forward to being in His presence forever and ever.

CONTENTS

ACKNOWLEDGMENTS

I want to thank my wonderful and gracious wife Carol who has supported me in this ministry with sacrifice, enthusiasm, encouragement, and accountability. Most of all, she has been a constant blessing because of her willingness to listen. I was always sharing with her the truths God had been teaching me as I studied His word and wrote this book. It consumed many hours. Thank you, Carol and I deeply love you.

I want to thank my son Gregory R. Jones for volunteering to be the primary editor of this important book. Without his time and effort in painstakingly and meticulously going over every word and every sentence checking and rechecking the sentence structure and grammar, I would not have been able to complete it. Thank you for your ministry to me. I love you my son.

I want to thank my other children, Krista, Matt, and Kara for their love for Christ and His Word and their willingness to live for Him. I love you all.

Introduction

This series of three books (Part 1,2,3) grew out of a desire to put the material in my main book on healing relationship through forgiveness into a format for small group study. As a result, the introductions are the same in all three books. This is primarily due to the essential nature of the content in our understanding of the truths found in each one. It also allows the books to be read and studied one after the other or to be studied independent of the other two. This provides more flexibility to the various individuals, groups, churches, and organizations who wish to use it.

After Moses had received the Ten Commandments, the prophet and leader requested that God show him His glory. The Almighty explained to Moses that no human could see Him and live. Nevertheless, God would grant his request by allowing His servant Moses to experience the passing of His "goodness" by him and the actual viewing of the "backside of His glory." On the next morning, he stood upon a rock and called upon the name of the Lord. The Lord God descended in the form of a cloud, shielded Moses in the cleft of the rock, and covered him with His divine hand. As God displayed His divine glory visibly, He declared the many attributes of His supernatural, divine character.

In Exodus 34:6-7, Moses described this amazing moment and the words that he heard the Lord declare about Himself. The prophet recorded, "Yahweh [I AM THAT I AM] passed by before him...he proclaimed, 'Yahweh! Yahweh, a merciful and gracious God, slow to anger...abundant in His loving kindness and truth, keeping loving kindness for thousands, forgiving iniquity and disobedience and sin.'" A book that is written on healing relationships through forgiveness by its nature must begin with the proclamation that the God of the universe is not only the merciful, gracious, patient, loving, kind, truth-filled, just, and righteous Lord but an Almighty deity who "forgives iniquity, transgressions, and sin." This Lord God announced that He is a "forgiving" God.

This by no means negates the fact that He is also a just and righteous one; therefore, this forgiveness comes with a price that had to be paid. So, He sent His Son to die to pay the penalty for our sins in order to pour out His forgiveness upon all mankind. Through faith in Jesus Christ, men and women experience the full extent of His forgiveness that was proclaimed to Moses many years ago on that mountain top. Once this has occurred in our lives, we are to live for Him. We are to act like Him, and we are to obey Him. One of the critical ways in which God desires His forgiven people to live for, act like, and obey Him is *to forgive others as we are forgiven*. This is the key point of these books. As the Lord God has forgiven us and healed our relationship with Him, He requires us to forgive and heal our relationships with others. This is found in several passages in the Scriptures. Two of them are mentioned by our Lord and one from the apostle Paul. All three clearly explain the important truth that relationships are to be "reconciled" and "restored" to "gain back" one's brother, sister, or neighbor. This is done primarily through forgiveness.

In Matthew 5, the Lord Jesus discusses the heart attitudes people in His kingdom should possess. After speaking of anger, the Lord presents a general principle of living in His kingdom on earth. In verses 23-24, He explains, "If therefore you are offering your gift at the altar, and there remember that your brother has anything against you, leave your gift there before the altar, and go your way. First be reconciled to your brother, and then come and offer your gift." The Greek word translated "reconciled" means "to make changes." It originates from a Greek root word that was a banking term meaning "to render accounts the same." There would be a discrepancy between two bank ledgers, and all the mistakes would have to be found and corrected in order for them to agree. We express this between people as "being on the same page." The Lord Jesus indicates that the Father desires His people to come to Him fully reconciled with each other. If we, as Christians, know that someone harbors something against us, we are to take the initiative and go to them and reconcile with them. We should not wait for them to come to us. We take our responsibility and go to them. We must once again "settle accounts." They have the same responsibility.

In Matthew 18, Jesus discusses those who are sinning in the church and what all believers should do. In verse 15, the Lord commands, "If your brother sins against you, go, show him his fault between you and him alone. If he listens to you, you have gained back your brother." The Greek word translated "gain" refers "to obtaining or securing something." When a relationship is restored, we gain back everything that the other parties contributed. In this particular case, we have something against our brother, rather than the reverse. If this does happen, we are to take the initiative and confront our brother or sister to gain him or her back and restore the relationship. So whether someone has something against us or we have something against someone else, the procedure is essentially the same. Christians must take the initiative and reconcile with them.

The third passage involves the restoration of a sinning brother in the church. In Galatians 6, Paul opens the chapter with an explanation of how to help a sinning saint. In verse one, Paul asserts, "Brothers, even if a man is caught in some fault, you who are spiritual must restore such a one." The Greek word translated "restore" means "to render fit, sound, or complete; to mend or repair what has been broken." The word is used of a physically broken fishing net. In Mark 1:19

and Matthew 4:21, when Jesus called James and John into ministry with Him, they were in the process of "mending" their fishing nets. They were mending the holes in their net so the fish would not fall through. This restoration could easily involve a conflict between two people. The holes in their relationship need to be mended. This process involves healing relationships through forgiveness. These passages will be referred to as you read.

These books are my original works on reconciliation and forgiveness. It is not based on other books that I have read and simply collated. To produce this work, I carefully read through the entire New Testament verse by verse. Then, I meticulously perused the Old Testament paying particular attention to the Psalms and Proverbs. As I read, categories were built from the individual passages, rather than a set of preconceived notions. These numerous categories became the individual biblical principles found in every chapter. Each passage was studied in its historical, grammatical, and scriptural contexts. After this, I compared my interpretations with those of past and present scholars. After this study, I have attempted to follow these biblical principles in my own personal life and also utilize them in my pastoral counseling practice. I have seen the Holy Spirit use them to transform relationships of all kinds.

One last thought. At the end of each chapter, I discuss a counseling experience. Due to confidentiality, none of these are based on one particular counseling situation. Instead, I have mixed together common elements I have seen, details from books and films, bits from my own life and the lives of people I have known, and thoughts from my imagination to create a situation where the biblical principles discussed in the chapters can fully be applied. These are composites of real life situations. Read, learn, and apply. I commend you to the Lord and His Word (Acts 20:32).

Chapter 1

Ask Others Next

When we have sinned against others, one of the most difficult things to do is to ask for forgiveness. Perhaps, we are too proud to humble ourselves. Maybe, we are fearful of their response. We could even be simply too ashamed to face them. This is a step that is often ignored, and we may even pretend the sin never happened. We simply go about our business as if everything is fine when it is not. Herein lies the problem: if we cannot do this with God, our Father, then we cannot do this with others. The Scriptures do not allow it. Whether the other person requests it or not, the Lord does.

A Typical Scenario

Have you ever had or perhaps heard a conversation like this concerning a father and his teenage daughter? He says, "I am not going to ask for forgiveness. (Wife responds.) Yes, I know I accused her and punished her for the dent in the car. (Wife responds.) I know now that the neighbor did it and not her, but I do not like her attitude. (Wife responds.) No! I will not ask her for forgiveness. Period!" Even though this typical father was wrong, he does not want to admit it. He refuses to ask his daughter for forgiveness. Have you ever felt that way about someone you know or love? Have you refused to ask for forgiveness from someone you have wronged?

The answer is obvious, we all have experienced this. Since he is a Christian, we know it will not be long before the Holy Spirit convicts him, and he will reconcile with his daughter.

If he does not, this will create a wall in their relationship. As he does this over and over again, this wall will grow taller and taller. Eventually, there will no longer be a relationship. All our relationships can fall victim to our unwillingness to ask for forgiveness and to reconcile. In the introduction to this book, I referred to three important passages indicating that God has only one way to restore relationships, and it is through forgiveness (Matthew 5:23-24; 18:15; Galatians 6:1).

A Scriptural Principle

The first principle is both obvious and natural. It is "we must reconcile our relationship (see Introduction) with those we have sinned against by asking for forgiveness." This next important step simply involves asking for and then receiving forgiveness. This will occur first with God, then with the others involved. This was described in 1 John 1:9, "If we confess our sins, he is faithful and righteous to forgive us the sins, and to cleanse us from all unrighteousness with God." These Greek verbs are in the present tense which indicates continuous action in present time. In our relationship to the Father through Jesus Christ, we are continually confessing our sins, and the Lord God is continually forgiving our sins. This describes the life of a believer with God: confessing and forgiving. This does not describe the full forgiveness on the cross (Romans 8:1); instead it explains relational forgiveness people bestow on each other as they fellowship together.

A Biblical Explanation

As Christians, we are constantly confessing, and God is constantly forgiving. It is the same way in our relationships with others. We are to behave in our relationship with others as we do with God: confessing and forgiving. In Luke 17:3-4, this is exactly what Jesus affirms when He says, "Be careful. If your brother sins against you, rebuke him. If he repents [confesses and asks for forgiveness], forgive him. If he sins against you seven times in the day, and seven times returns, saying, 'I repent,' you shall forgive him." This confessing is the admitting of what we specifically did wrong. Then there is a mourning and sorrow over the sin. This leads to the final stage which involves turning in the opposite direction from what we did. We do this with God, and then we do the same with others.

This asking for forgiveness of those we have wronged is so obvious and is such a normal part of life. It is woven into our very fabric as human beings. When we are transgressed, we expect the person to come to us and ask for forgiveness. In Romans 2, Paul is discussing the conscience, and its place in the judgment of man. He explains that within people is a law God puts within their hearts, and they will be judged according to that law. In verse 15, Paul describes it, "In that they show the work of the law written in their hearts, their conscience testifying with them, and their thoughts among themselves accusing or else excusing them." When we hurt, or harm a person, we will have a natural desire to ask for forgiveness because it is written on our hearts.

When people sin against others, their consciences begin to condemn them for the transgression and exhort them to ask for forgiveness. Why? It is in their nature. In verse 14, Paul asserts, "For when Gentiles who don't have the law do by nature the things of the law, these, not having the law, are a law to themselves." Asking for forgiveness is one of those natural things inside us. It is a law or rule within our nature. When we wrong people, we know innately that we must ask them for their forgiveness. When people wrong us, then we expect them to ask for forgiveness. This is so obvious that it barely needs discussion.

This concept of "sinning against" someone is found in several places in the Bible. One example is found in the life of Abraham. While living in the land of Gerar, he was afraid that the king would be attracted to his wife and kill him to take her for himself. So Abraham asked Sarah to tell the king that he was her brother which she did. When the king took Sarah, as Abraham had predicted, his life was spared. Then God stepped in and stopped the king before he could violate her. The Lord told the king the truth about Abraham and closed the wombs of Abimelech's wife and female servants until he rectified the situation. In Genesis 20:9, Moses writes, "Then Abimelech [the king] called Abraham, and said to him, 'What have you done to us? How have I sinned against you, that you have brought on me and on my kingdom a great sin? You have done deeds to me that ought not to be done!'" Abimelech questioned Abraham as to how the king had "sinned against" him. Notice, this concept of "sinning against" others was a truth that was natural to all people.

Another example is found in the life of Jeremiah. When the Chaldeans were about to defeat Judah, King Zedekiah asked the prophet to inquire of the Lord and find out if the nation would be defeated. Some of his princes thought the prophet was a Chaldean sympathizer, and so they arrested him and imprisoned him. When the king called for Jeremiah, he asked the king what he had done wrong which deserved imprisonment. Jeremiah 37:18 describes the incident in these words, "Moreover Jeremiah said to king Zedekiah, 'Wherein have I sinned against you, or against your servants, or against this people, that you have put me in prison?'" The prophet attempts to ascertain exactly what he had done to this king. Notice again, Jeremiah calls it "sinning against" him, his servants, or people. Neither of these men needed to ask for forgiveness because they had done nothing wrong. Yet, both examples describe this concept of "sinning against" someone.

This companion concept of "asking for forgiveness" once someone is sinned against is also found in Scripture. After Pharaoh had refused to listen to Moses and let God's people go, the land was overtaken by swarms of locusts. Pharaoh responded immediately by repenting of his rash actions. In Exodus 10:16-17, Moses described it in these words, "Then Pharaoh called for Moses and Aaron in haste, and he said, 'I have sinned against Yahweh your God, and against you. Now therefore please forgive my sin again, and pray to Yahweh your God, that he may also take away from me this death.'" Here is a clear example of what this "asking for forgiveness" looks like, though it is from such a hard-hearted man. Pharaoh admits his transgression against God first and then Moses.

In 1 Samuel 25, David encounters a foolish man named Nabal who refused to be hospitable toward David and his men while they were on a journey. David had been careful to make sure his men had treated Nabal's men properly and then asked for some provisions for their travels. This was an important cultural practice, since there were very few inns and places to eat on the road. Nabal, though very wealthy, refused to even acknowledge David. This was an offensive act on Nabal's part, and David was extremely offended. He immediately commanded his men to take up their swords to defend their honor.

When Nabal's wife, Abigail, discovered this humiliation of David, she quickly took action to protect her husband. She went out to meet David and took full responsibility for her husband's actions. She pleaded for forgiveness for the both of them. In 1 Samuel 25:23-24, the author describes their encounter, "When Abigail saw David, she hurried and got off of her donkey, and fell before David on her face, and bowed herself to the ground. She fell at his feet, and said, 'On me, my lord, on me be the blame! Please let your servant

9

speak in your ears. Hear the words of your servant.'" Abigail admitted the transgression and displayed her sorrow over the whole incident. Then she provided David with all the rations that they needed for their journey. What gifts! This demonstrated her repentance as she turned in the opposite direction from what had been done. Ultimately, God judged foolish Nabal by taking his life, and this righteous woman became David's wife.

The parables of Jesus were made-up stories of the many common life experiences of the people. Jesus utilized them to teach particular truths about the kingdom of God. We can learn what life was like at the time merely by observing the interactions of the many characters in these parables. In the parable known as "The Parable of the Prodigal Son," we have an example of this principle of "asking for forgiveness" when one transgresses another. After the son had taken his portion of his inheritance and squandered it all, he repents of this sin. He returns to his father to beg him for forgiveness. He explained that he no longer deserved treatment as a son and requested he be hired as a day laborer, so he could pay back all he had wasted.

In Luke 15:21, Jesus described the meeting of the father and son in these words, "He arose, and came to his father. But while he was still far off, his father saw him, and was moved with compassion, and ran, and fell on his neck, and kissed him." The father showed his son great compassion, mercy, and grace. His arms were open to him. Then Jesus speaks of the repentant son's urgent request for his father's full forgiveness, "The son said to him, 'Father, I have sinned against heaven, and in your sight. I am no longer worthy to be called your son.'" This wayward son recognized that he had sinned both against God and against his father. He then asks his father for forgiveness. We are to do the same when we transgress others.

Paul himself alludes to this practice when he rebukes the Corinthians for accusing him of preaching to them in order to ascertain money. It was exactly the opposite. He was so concerned that they might think this that he worked in his tent-making trade and used the funds from other churches to support himself. Then he shared the gospel with them. In 2 Corinthians 12:13, he sarcastically questions, "For what is there in which you were made inferior to the rest of the assemblies, unless it is that I myself was not a burden to you? Forgive me this wrong." He requests them to forgive him for a wrong which he did not do, but they had thought he had done. Though he is using sarcasm to make his point, we have a simple example of this principle of "asking for forgiveness" when someone has been wronged by us.

At times, people are afraid to ask for forgiveness because they might not receive a kind and gracious reaction from the person they transgressed. This does not matter. The reaction he or she has is entirely up to the Lord God. It only matters that we accept the responsibility for the sins we committed. Be forewarned, it may take some time to prepare ourselves fully for the confessing and repenting, and it may take time for the person we have wronged to forgive.

That's fine! This is one of the many reasons the Christian life is called a walk because it involves one step at a time (Galatians 5:16). Why? The sin principle within all believers is strong and influential (Romans 7:14). If we are the ones who have wronged someone, our flesh may want to pretend it never happened and move on. It may require some serious time in the word and prayer to ask for forgiveness. If we do engage in this process, we can expect a slow and meticulous decline in every aspect of our relationship. How do people live with others who can never utter these important and necessary words, "I am sorry?" The other will feel that they are always taking the blame which will wear them out.

An Ancient Portrait

This process is so aptly demonstrated in the life of Joseph. His brothers were reluctant to ask for forgiveness when they sinned against Joseph. This story is found in Genesis 37-50. Joseph was hated by his brothers because he was the favored son and had two disturbing dreams. These dreams indicated that his brothers would bow down, honor, and serve him one day. As a result, they sold him into slavery and Joseph was then purchased by Potiphar, the captain of Pharaoh's bodyguard.

After being accused of rape and being thrown in prison, Joseph interpreted the dreams of two Egyptians. One was restored to Pharaoh's court and informed him of Joseph's gift when the emperor wanted two dreams interpreted. The Pharaoh explained the dreams to Joseph and begged him for the interpretations from his God. This favored son of Jacob predicted that there would be seven years of plenty and seven years of famine in the land. He recommended that Pharaoh assign someone to gather grain into storehouses during the time of plenty and then distribute it during the time of famine. Pharaoh took his advice and appointed him over the entire kingdom at the age of thirty.

Several years later, his father Jacob began to experience the famine back in the land of Canaan. Jacob sent his sons to Pharaoh's court to buy grain. All went except Benjamin who was Joseph's blood brother. When his brothers arrived to purchase grain from Joseph, they did not recognize him. Yet, Joseph realized that he was in the presence of his brothers. He had to excuse himself to weep in private. Though Moses does not explain the tears, they appeared to be tears of joy. Though they had sold him into slavery, Joseph knew God's higher purpose for allowing it to happen. He had already forgiven his brothers for what they had done; even though, they had not asked for forgiveness. Isn't this what God does continually in our lives, since the entire debt of our sins were nailed to the cross (Colossians 2:14)?

Through a series of schemes, Joseph forced his brothers to bring Benjamin and eventually their father Jacob to Egypt. Finally, he revealed himself. After this, Jacob was brought to Egypt. His family was given a choice piece of land, and life in Egypt began. After a long period of time, Jacob eventually died. Now the brothers became fearful because they had not reconciled with Joseph. They had never acknowledged their evil before him, nor had they asked him for forgiveness. In Genesis 50:15, Moses describes it in this way, "When Joseph's brothers saw that their father was dead, they said, 'It may be that Joseph will hate us, and will fully pay us back for all of the evil which we did to him.'" They were scared of Joseph, so they sent a message asking for forgiveness. In verse 16 and the first part of 17, they claim that their father Jacob had wanted them to tell Joseph to forgive them. We do not know whether Jacob had actually said this, but it seems obvious that they were fearful that their brother was going to put them to death.

Then the brothers finally did what they should have done from the beginning - ask for forgiveness. Moses continues, "'Now please forgive the disobedience of your brothers, and their sin, because they did evil to you. Now, please forgive the disobedience of the servants of the God of your father." Here they bring God into the picture and beg for forgiveness which is what He would want them to do. After this, they both wept in each other's presence, Joseph granted them his forgiveness and explained the Lord's purpose in it all. Joseph had to experience all of this to bring him to a position that he could save the entire nation of Israel who was not yet born but still in his loins and those of his brother's. He also could deliver others on earth who came to buy grain from Egypt.

We do not know if Jacob had actually requested Joseph to forgive them or whether they lied to appease Joseph's anger. However, we do know that they did ask for forgiveness and humble themselves in confession, repentance, and sorrow before their brother Joseph.

Sometimes, the confession and repentance of people can be less than perfect but real and genuine. Again, we are all battling the flesh. Notice, they sent a message. There are times we have difficulty asking for forgiveness face to face. This is perfectly fine. A card, a letter, or even a text asking for forgiveness is very appropriate. Remember, much of the New Testament was written as letters. What could be better confirmation of the appropriateness of writing letters than this? Though I would like to give a caution, some people we have wronged may desire a face to face reconciliation. This should be granted, if possible. What a great illustration of our principle of asking someone for forgiveness. So, if we have a broken relationship with our spouse, partner, parent, child, friend, neighbor, co-worker, fellow student, or even an acquaintance, then we must go to them, ask for forgiveness, and reconcile. This is God's only process for restoration.

A Modern Anecdote

Sometime ago, a man entered my office in an angry rage. He wanted equal custody of his children, but his ex-wife had moved them to another city. This would not allow them to share custody on a rotating weekly basis. I inquired as to the salvation of both him and his ex-wife. He indicated that they were both saved but not living the Christian life the way they knew God had wanted. They divorced, and both found someone else and just as quickly married. There were four children involved of various ages, and they were having a myriad of problems with them at home and in school. He

14

wanted more access to them so he could be the father they needed, and the ex-wife was angry at him over the marriage and didn't want to give him any more time.

After several sessions, it was obvious to all of us that they had no biblical reason to end the marriage. They realized that they divorced over insignificant issues which had never been resolved. They let these simply built up over time until they claimed they were no longer "in love." This led to all the other problems including the custody issues. Since they were already married to someone else, they could not reconcile the relationship. Yet, they still had a relationship as mother and father. Their children needed a stable environment in both homes. This stability must come by aligning their new lives as close to the Lord's biblical blueprint for the family as possible. I asked each individually if they thought the other ex-spouse was a good parent. Each agreed.

As a result, the first aspect of their lives which must align more fully with the Scriptures was the children's access to both parents. Numerous times in the book of Proverbs and elsewhere, the inspired writers mention the teaching and training of both mother and father (Proverbs 1:8; 4:3; 6:20; 10:1; 15:20; 23:25; 30:17). So the custody was legally changed to rotating weeks. Since discipline is the critical issue in the lives of children, they should together establish four or five general rules with similar consequences for both homes. We worked on other parts of this new custody agreement and living plan that would stabilize both environments for these children. Children do not stop being children, when parent's divorce. They must still be trained and disciplined.

The next step in the process would require the greatest power from the Holy Spirit. They must reconcile with each other and the children. This could only be accomplished by each of them asking for forgiveness of the other and then the children. Both of them had sinned in the marriage, both had agreed to the divorce, and both had disrupted the lives of all their children by being unwilling to follow God's biblical blueprint. They must let the children know that the way they are living was not God's blueprint, but through His grace and His mercy He would work in spite of it. This way they would not add this broken model to their own repertoire of the many actions they could take when they had difficulties in their marriages. This healing process would also lessen the children's own wounds from the divorce as they entered their adolescent and adult lives. After asking forgiveness of each other, each parent sat in my office with each individual child. The father went first and then the mother.

It was a beautiful and supernatural experience for all involved. Both parents humbled themselves and asked for forgiveness from each child individually. Each one lovingly responded in their own way, "Yes, Daddy, I forgive you" and "Yes, Mommy, I forgive you." Then each was asked if they had something to confess to the parents concerning the wrong responses they may have made at home or in school in response to their parent's divorce (according to their age and understanding).

Each admitted that they were misbehaving and asked them for forgiveness and made a commitment "to be better." As each one spoke, I was praying and prompting them as necessary. Then we met together with the children and the new step-parents and explained the new stable living plan they would have. The joy on their faces was so rewarding. They looked at both parents and thanked them for trying so hard to make things right again for them. These new families had finally been reconciled through God's forgiveness. It was wonderful to watch God's Holy Spirit bring much joy, peace, and unity to the families. Of course, this was just the beginning of the work that needed to be done.

A Personal Response

Dear Heavenly Father,

   While I was learning the biblical principles in this chapter, I recognize that I have not asked (add name) for forgiveness for the transgressions I have committed against (add name). First, I am so sorry for (list transgressions) that I committed against (add name). Please help me have the courage to go to him (her) and ask him for forgiveness. Help me to honor and glorify You in my relationship with (add name) and follow your Word. I pray this in the name of Jesus. Amen.

Chapter 2

Humbly Make Restitution

Once we have asked others for forgiveness, we should consider another important step which is to make restitution if necessary. Though it is quite intuitive, often it is neglected. Why? We think this step is a part of forgiveness, rather than repentance. We suppose that we should make restitution to somehow influence or persuade them to forgive us. We also expect others to make restitution to us before we will truly forgive them. Yet, the Scriptures teach that we should simply forgive. Nothing is added to that anywhere in the Bible. So, restitution is really a way of demonstrating true repentance and may also be a part of our consequences. .

A Typical Scenario

Have you ever had or heard a conversation with someone that went something like this? You or they are mopping the floor and commenting to someone, "This is difficult. I never realized how hard housework can be. Yesterday was a house cleaning day for my wife (husband) and me. To be honest, I really did not want to clean up. So I got up late and took a really long time getting ready, but that didn't work. When she (he) told me to come and help, we got into an argument. It wasn't long before the conviction of the Holy Spirit came."

"First, I went to God and asked for His forgiveness; then I went to my wife (husband) and humbly asked for her (his) forgiveness, but I couldn't stop there. I felt so sorry, I had to make restitution. So I am doing yesterday's housework, and then I realized how poorly I had behaved. So, I decided that

I would add some extra cleaning to what she (he) wanted me to do, so I am adding two additional things."

A Scriptural Principle

Now we come to the second principle. It is "we should demonstrate repentance by making restitution." The concept of restitution involves primarily doing something we should have done, or maybe replacing something we took or broke, perhaps retracting something we should not have said, or redoing something we should not have done in the first place. Restitution is not penance to make-up for any of our transgressions, so someone we wronged will forgive us. God does not require this from us because that it is considered "works." As a result, forgiveness is based on His grace, not any works. We should forgive someone who transgresses us based on God's grace. Then, someone we transgress forgives us based also on God's grace. This is God's way.

A Biblical Explanation

Restitution is not a part of the forgiveness process of the person wronged but a part of the repentance process of the person who did the wrong. It is to demonstrate repentance to the wronged party and ourselves. This process may also be a part of the consequences of our wrongdoing and will definitely aid in the repair of a broken relationship. For us to forgive or be forgiven, it is not biblically required. Christians are to forgive whether restitution comes or not. When we are sorry for what we did, it is natural to want to fix the wrong.

In the Old Testament, as the people of Israel journeyed through the wilderness, the Lord was preparing them to be a nation devoted to Him and to His will. He set certain laws that He wanted Israel to follow as His nation and people. These laws were either moral, legal, ceremonial, or even a combination of two or all three. The Lord also determined that different misdeeds, both intentional and unintentional, would have different consequences which depended on the specific actions. Most of these misdeeds involved making restitution to the one transgressed. This was to be done as a manner of life, whether a judgment (legal actions) was given or not (personal actions). In either case, since God was also transgressed a sacrifice had to be made to the priest.

In Leviticus 6:4, God declares, "Then it shall be, if he has sinned, and is guilty, he shall restore that which he took by robbery, or the thing which he has gotten by oppression, or the deposit which was committed to him, or the lost thing which he found." The Lord begins with a list of wrongdoing that needs to be recompensed. The most important issue is that it actually occurred. Since these are national laws, then the person needs to be found guilty. If it is a personal act then the person must admit he did it. This is the confession step we have discussed. Then the Lord lists robbery which is stealing something that one does not own. He mentions extortion which is forcing someone to give you something that he owns. The third is keeping a deposit wrongfully which means one made a commitment to do something if another put a deposit down, but he did not do it. He must return the deposit. Another grievance may involve someone borrowing something, losing it, and never replacing it.

In the beginning of verse 5, the Lord continues with the last one, "Or anything about which he has sworn falsely." This is a person who was a false witness, or who lied and committed slander or libel. Then God explains exactly what He desires to be done to make restitution, "He shall restore it even in full, and shall add a fifth part more to it." The person who must make restitution should give the same amount back plus twenty percent more. Then God provides the exact time table for this to occur, "To him to whom it belongs he shall give it, in the day of his being found guilty." As soon as people are found guilty for the transgression or in a personal case admit it, they should begin the restitution process. This demonstrates repentance, acceptance of the consequences and the desire to restore the relationship.

In Numbers 5:6-7, the Lord God reiterates His commands concerning restitution again. Here God summarizes this important truth. In verse 6, God commands, "Speak to the children of Israel: 'When a man or woman commits any sin that men commit, so as to trespass against Yahweh, and that soul is guilty." God speaks of any transgression that involves another person in anyway which is also a transgression against God. Then He explains what they are to do. In verse 7, God explains, "Then he shall confess his sin which he has done, and he shall make restitution for his guilt in full, and add to it the fifth part of it, and give it to him in respect of whom he has been guilty." God's people were to give back what they took or lost, tell the truth if they lied, and add a fifth part. They would add twenty percent more, if possible.

Previously, God had indicated other situations that may require more than twenty percent plus the replacement or replacement amount. In Exodus 22:1-14 the restitution can double or quadruple for certain actions. The point is that the nation of Israel was bound by restitution. This was their national law and their everyday practice. Today, numerous governments may require restitution for certain acts. If they do, then we make restitution as we obey the government as servants of God (Romans 13:1-4).

So, the Old Testament not only required restitution in its laws but also provides several examples of this. One is an incident involving Abimelech and Abraham. Though this king did not actually violate Sarah, he did take the wife of a prophet of God into his own household with the intention of doing so. As the king or not, Abimelech had no right to take multiple women into his household for his own pleasure. Abraham was in such fear of Abimelech's evil and lecherous methods, he lied about his wife. The Lord God punished his household until Abimelech made restitution.

In Genesis 20:14-16, Moses describes it, "Abimelech took sheep and cattle, male servants and female servants, and gave them to Abraham, and restored Sarah, his wife, to him. Abimelech said, 'Behold, my land is before you. Dwell where it pleases you.' To Sarah he said, 'Behold, I have given your brother a thousand pieces of silver. Behold, it is for you a covering of the eyes to all that are with you. In front of all you are vindicated.'" The restitution was to demonstrate his repentance and to show the world that Sarah had never been violated by Him. It was also consequences from God that he would have to accept. Then Abraham prayed for Abimelech and God once again opened the wombs of his wife and his female servants.

Another illustration of this restitution is found in another story from the Bible. This was the spurning of David by Nabal when he would not provide the hospitality that the culture at the time demanded of him. When Abigail asked for forgiveness, she provided restitution. In 1 Samuel 25:27, the author records, "Now this present which your servant has brought to my lord, let it be given to the young men who follow my lord." We discover from 1 Samuel 25:18 what this "present" was, "Then Abigail hurried and took two hundred loaves of bread, two bottles of wine, five sheep ready dressed, five seahs of parched grain, one hundred clusters of raisins, and two hundred cakes of figs, and laid them on donkeys." This restitution would have more than provided for all their needs. Also, this restitution built a relationship between Abigail and David that would later blossom into a marriage when she became a widow at God's hand. In 1 Samuel 25:32-33, David responded with this blessing, "David said to Abigail, 'Blessed is Yahweh, the God of Israel, who sent you today to meet me!'" He gives tribute to the Lord God then to Abigail. He adds, "Blessed is your discretion, and blessed are you, who have kept me today from blood guiltiness, and from avenging myself with my own hand."

When God's people were released from captivity, they returned to the land under the leadership of Nehemiah. Sometime later, Nehemiah discovered that the Jewish people left behind were charging huge amounts of interest (called usury) to loan people money to eat and supply some basic needs. As a result, they even took some of their own people as slaves who could not pay them back. Nehemiah was livid and called the people together and rebuked them strongly. As they repented, they then made restitution. In Nehemiah 5:10-13, the author communicates, "'I likewise, my brothers and my servants, lend them money and grain. Please let us stop this usury."

First, Nehemiah rebukes them. Then he cries out, "Please restore to them, even today, their fields, their vineyards, their olive groves, and their houses, also the hundredth part of the money, and of the grain, the new wine, and the oil, that you are charging them." After he entreats them to make restitution, they responded, "Then they said, 'We will restore them, and will require nothing of them; so will we do, even as you say.'"

To make sure this occurred, he demanded an oath, "Then I called the priests, and took an oath of them, that they would do according to this promise. Also, I shook out my lap, and said, 'So may God shake out every man from his house, and from his labor, that doesn't perform this promise;

even thus be he shaken out, and emptied.'" With this oath, Nehemiah proclaimed a curse, and the people answered, "All the assembly said, 'Amen,' and praised Yahweh. The people did according to this promise." After their repentance for the usury, Nehemiah required them to make restitution in full by returning everything they had taken. The account doesn't mention whether he required an additional amount or not.

When we come to the New Testament, Rome ruled over the Jewish nation. The Jews were allowed to enforce certain of their laws, and the Romans the more serious ones. Both Jewish law and Roman law had elements of restitution. For Jews, it was still a powerful cultural mandate and expected. There is no specific command by Jesus or the other inspired writers to make restitution in every instance. Yet, it certainly appears to be a practice in normal Jewish life. The story of the two debtors in Matthew 18:23-35, both offered to make restitution for their debts, though neither was able to.

Many are familiar with the story of the repentance of the prodigal son. After this son had consumed his portion of the inheritance, even before his father had died, he experienced great remorse. He then decided that he would return to his loving father and beg for forgiveness. As he did this, he asked his father for a job as a day laborer. Why? He desired to pay back all he had taken. He wanted to make restitution for the squandered money. Jesus describes the son's desire to make this restitution in Luke 15:19. He says, "I am no more worthy to be called your son. Make me as one of your hired servants." Yet, the prodigal son was not required to make any restitution because the father did not desire it. This was a picture of God, the Father, who does not require restitution from us, since Christ paid for the debt of our sins on the cross. Next, Jesus accepted it from Zacchaeus as a sign of his repentance. He did not hinder his restitution attempt.

An Ancient Portrait

The classic biblical example of making restitution is the tax-collector Zacchaeus when he meets Jesus, repents, and receives the Lord. The story of Zacchaeus is found in Luke 19:1-10. Jesus Christ entered the town of Jericho on His way to Jerusalem for the yearly Passover with a large crowd. This important city was on the main route to Jerusalem, and all the pilgrims would be traveling through this town also. The citizens of Jericho would have heard that Jesus had raised Lazarus from the dead and would have come out to see Him. The town would have been teeming with people.

Amid this crowd, a rich and powerful tax collector named Zacchaeus entered the scene. It was the law that once these officials charged the people what Rome had designated, they could then charge any fee they desired. As a result, these men gouged the people and became rich. If they did not pay, the tax collectors would try and intimidate them into paying through threats or physical force. He was one of the "chief" tax collectors, so he also received a percentage of the amount of taxes collected by every tax collector under him. This made him even richer. These people were hated by the Jews. Why? They extorted the Jewish people and worked for the Romans. The Hebrews called them "sinners." This was the lowest class of people in their country. They were unclean, defiled, and outcasts. These evil ones were to be completely avoided and not allowed to enter the home of any Jew or the synagogue. Zacchaeus was a member of this group. He had heard that the Lord Jesus was in town and wanted to see Him. Why? We can discern this from what happened.

This hated man was honestly seeking true salvation as the Holy Spirit was working powerfully in his heart. The Spirit was convicting Him of His sin and leading Him to the Jesus, the Savior. He had one "big" problem. He was small, a little man vying for a place to see in a large crowd. So Zacchaeus decided to run ahead of Jesus and find himself a place to see this extraordinary man. He climbed up into a sycamore or perhaps a mulberry tree because these had short trunks and long branches which made them easy to climb. When the Messiah came to the place where Zacchaeus was located, something remarkable happened.

The Lord stopped, looked him straight in the eyes, and called him by his name. Jesus knew Zacchaeus, who he was and all that he had done. He said, "Come down, I will stay with you today." Jesus decided to lodge with him overnight. This tax collector hurried down and received the Lord Jesus joyfully into his home. Zacchaeus stood before Jesus and repented saying, "Behold, Lord, half of my goods I will give to the poor." The Lord Christ's recognition of Zacchaeus was miraculous and obviously the final action that convinced this searching but scorned man that Jesus was the Christ. It obviously led to his act of repentance. In his repentance, we see a very dramatic reaction to receiving Christ as Savior and Lord. Zacchaeus first declares he will give half of his money away. Why? Money had been his idol. Now, Jesus was His Lord, and he wouldn't serve money any longer.

Then Zacchaeus committed himself to making restitution. This tax collector had essentially stolen and cheated so many people out of so much money that he declared, "If I have wrongfully exacted anything of anyone, I restore four times as much." He saw the awfulness of his greed which had led him to oppress many innocent people and absolutely had to compensate them even more than required. The Lord saw this dramatic response and declared, "Today, salvation has come to this house." This was a true son of Abraham in the Spirit now not one of the flesh alone. The Lord Jesus doesn't correct Zacchaeus regarding the restitution but affirms it as a demonstration of his strong repentance. Does not restitution make sense in not only displaying one's true repentance but also in rebuilding the broken relationship?

It is such a typical occurrence in our lives. If we break someone's stuff, we have it fixed. If we eat someone's pie by mistake, we replace it. The conscience demands a proper demonstration of repentance through restitution, and this humble action will aid in the crucial process of restoring relationships. It is not commanded in the New Testament, but it was definitely an Old Testament law and pattern. Also, it makes good sense. Sometimes, it is hard to take the necessary steps to make restitution, but we will never be disappointed by its supernatural effects. More importantly, it always demonstrates repentance and honors our glorious Lord.

A Modern Anecdote

We live in a world of credit cards and personal loans. If we so desire, we can simply purchase anything by sliding a card into a machine, and it is ours. Unfortunately, the money must be paid back with interest, and this is a source of much conflict between couples in their marriages. One such couple came to my counseling office to speak about this very issue. From the start, the couple had decided that the wife ought to be a "stay at home mom" and handle the actual payment of the bills while her husband worked. The problem started when her only child, a daughter, entered high school. Before that time, mom was quite involved with her school. When the high school years began, her daughter simply did not want her mother around. The wife suddenly had a large amount of time on her hands. To fill the time, she developed a practice of going shopping. At first, she merely window shopped, but it was not very long before she was noticing the many sales she was missing out on.

In fact, she felt like the family was losing money as she perused the sales, but did not buy. So she decided to utilize the family's credit cards to make the purchases that they needed in order to take advantage of the numerous sales and save money. It soon turned into the things she wanted for herself. Within months, their credit cards were maxed out. At first, she was panicked. Then an idea came to her. She would borrow money from the college savings account earmarked for their daughter and then quickly and quietly pay it back. At first, it started with small withdrawals. Then, she did not have enough to pay for all the minimum credit card payments, and so the wife had to leave the deficit in the savings.

This happened more often than she had anticipated. Over a matter of time, the savings account was depleted, and her daughter's future at college was in jeopardy. It finally came to a head when the daughter asked her father if she could use her college money to hire a tutor to help her prepare for her college entrance exams. Since she would be taking these exams in another year, she wanted to be ready. When her father went to the bank to make the appropriate withdrawal, the teller explained to him that he had insufficient funds.

He could not believe what he had just heard. This was impossible, so he demanded to see the bank manager. As she showed him the many withdrawals his wife had made over the past months, the husband squirmed in his seat. After humbly apologizing, the husband drove home furious with his "out of control" wife. He stomped in the house, shouted a series of unflattering and unholy words at her, and then he demanded an explanation.

A huge argument ensued. When their teenage daughter found out what her mother had done, she ran into her room and cried about her now grim future. Finally, the wife and mother confessed all that she had done. The hard part was over, she regretted her actions and desired reconciliation as did her husband and daughter. The husband and daughter responded with their own desire to help by taking on extra hours and paying off the credit card debt. After some time, everything was restored. Then, I encouraged the mother to take her extra time and use her spiritual gifts to minster to the saints and share the gospel. She now happily works at her church with young mothers (Titus 2:3-4).

A Personal Response

Dear Heavenly Father,

Your Holy Spirit has shown me that I have not fully made restitution for the transgressions I have committed toward (add name). I am truly sorry. Please give me the wisdom to discern what restitution would be appropriate and provide the commitment and courage to do it. I do desire to reconcile my relationship with (add name) for your honor and glory. I pray this in the name of Jesus. Amen.

Chapter 3

Accept the Consequences

Another step involves the willingness to accept all the consequences for what we have done. This truth can be seen in various relationships we have. Children living at home will have consequences for violating their parent's rules. At times, our spouses may desire to set up boundaries for some habitual sinful behavior we may have developed during the marriage (drunkenness, drug use, gambling, etc.). They may require us to seek help or take the risk of a break-up of the marriage. These are consequences of our sins.

The church is required to discipline its many members for unrepentant sins against the brethren (Matthew 18:17). We always find that our employers have rules and consequences for breaking them. Every society has a government which creates its laws and punishes its citizens for violating them. Even our friends may have to help us get back in line with them by providing consequences for our behavior towards them. In fact, every healthy relationship has boundaries and rules set up formally or informally with consequences for ones who refuse to respect the other member or members. God may intervene and have consequences of His own since we have also violated His laws. This chapter involves the discussion of these consequences and their importance.

A Typical Scenario

Imagine yourself involved in an intense time-consuming activity. You suddenly look at your clock, gasp, and scream, "Oh no, I forgot to pick up (insert name) at their activity. He (she) is going to be so angry at me. I came into the family room to retrieve my keys and had just a few extra minutes. Then I got started, and those minutes turned into an hour. I totally forgot to pick (insert name) up!" Suddenly, your flesh begins to flare up, and you think, "I'm in trouble, but I don't care. That is not my problem! Everybody makes mistakes. If I get the silent treatment or yelled at, then I will give it back to him (her)" Has this ever happened to you? It has to me. Sometimes, we do something wrong, but we refuse to accept the consequences. This is not what God desires.

A Scriptural Principle

We now come to principle number three. This principle is "we should accept whatever consequences that may result from our sin against God and others." Sin leads to a variety of consequences. When we travel back to the garden, God told Adam that if he disobeyed Him and ate of a particular tree, he would die. That is a consequence of sin. When Adam ate of the fruit, he died, not physically but spiritually and set in motion a myriad of consequences for that one act.

A Biblical Explanation

Why must there be consequences to almost everything we do? Scientists describe it as a simple case of cause and effect. To every action there is some kind of reaction or effect. The Bible describes it as a law of God set forth in His universe. In Galatians 5, Paul had just contrasted the fruits of the Spirit with the deeds of the flesh. In Galatians 6, to encourage the saints at Galatia to remain diligent in producing these fruits (doing good), he explains that the spiritual realm functions according to this cause and effect relationship. In verses 7-8, he utilizes a farming analogy to explain it. He writes, "Don't be deceived. God is not mocked, for whatever a man sows, that he will also reap. For he who sows to his own flesh will from the flesh reap corruption. But he who sows to the Spirit will from the Spirit reap eternal life."

Here the apostle describes a general principle of farming. If a farmer sows with good seeds, he will reap good crops; if he sows using bad seeds, he will reap bad crops. Whatever he sows, he will reap. Then Paul explains how this physical analogy applies to supernatural things. When Christians sin by sowing to the flesh, they reap corruption. When believers live righteously and sow to the Spirit, they reap eternal life. When we follow our lusts, they lead us to corrupt activities, not activities of eternal life. When we follow the Spirit, He leads us to activities having to do with eternal life.

The general principle is the same spiritually or physically: whatever we sow, we reap. Then he issues a strong entreaty in verse nine. He asserts, "Let us not be weary in doing good, for we will reap in due season, if we don't give up." True Christians can never give up in their striving for good. The reaping of blessings will come at the right time not only in this life but more importantly in the life to come. After Paul exhorted the Thessalonians to work hard as he did and not to depend on others for their livelihood, Paul entreats them with the same principle. In 2 Thessalonians 3:13, the apostle proclaims, "But you, brothers, don't be weary in doing well." This includes all relationships. Why? When we grow weary, the flesh becomes active and corrupt activities occur in our relationships.

How does this principle of sowing and reaping actually work in relationships? First, if we will sow good seeds in our relationships, it will reap blessings. If we sow bad seeds in our relationships, it will reap corruption. Sowing the fruits of the Spirit (love, joy, peace, patience, kindness, goodness, faith, gentleness, and self-control), will produce a thriving relationship. Sowing the deeds of the flesh (hatred, strife, immorality, jealousy, anger), will produce a deteriorating relationship. In our seeking forgiveness context, we have sown bad seeds into our relationships with people, and now we must reconcile with them. Since we sowed bad seed into the relationship, there will come some bad consequences. When we repent of the sin, we should still expect some of those consequences. This is often in the form of restitution. We may have to retract something we should not have said, do something we did not do, undo something we did, fix what we broke or even replace what we lost. Accepting these consequences demonstrates our repentance also. So, restitution could be one of the many ways we accept the consequences for our sins against others.

Another way we might have to accept the consequences for our sin is to allow the people transgressed to deal with our sin in the manner and time frame they may require, not the manner and time frame we may require. For example, if we make our spouses, parents, friends, neighbors, children, fellow students, or co-workers angry and they ignore us for a few days, we must accept this consequence for our action. They could need time to work out their responses to our sinful actions. If we violate a trust of our parents or spouses, we may have to check in with them more often. Perhaps, they will want everything we say to be verified for a while. These consequences ought to be accepted. It might not be something we would need to rebuild the trust, but they do. It is critical that they receive this assurance.

If we promised to do something that is important to a friend and we fail to do it, he or she may not rely on us for a while. They might even need for us to demonstrate we are reliable by proceeding through a series of steps so they may finally trust us again. It may differ completely from how we would handle the same issue, but it is part of accepting every one of the consequences. Often times, once believers have repented, they think no consequences are really necessary. A spouse will say to the other, "I told you I was sorry. You have to forgive me and drop it!" We will not allow people to be human and to experience all the feelings humans may feel when something evil is done against them. People need time to deal with the issue in a spiritual way themselves. They may react sinfully and need to deal with the Lord. If our sinful actions set into motion a wide range of sinful and non-sinful reactions to them from those we have transgressed, the consequences may be to allow them time to process all of it. This is the second reason that this acceptance is important.

The third reason accepting consequences is so critical to a relationship is that this is God's basic strategy to train us. If we refuse to accept the consequences for our sins, we are circumventing our learning process. Because God is a loving Father, He trains and disciplines us to act like Him and live in a holy way. This is called "sanctification." Accepting the many consequences for our actions will assist in the training process. In Hebrews 12:7, speaking of the numerous trials in the life of believers, the author declares, "It is for discipline that you endure. God deals with you as with children, for what son is there whom his father doesn't discipline?"

God brings trials into the lives of His children (some self-imposed) to train them. This is what a loving father will do. The Greek word translated "discipline" means "instruction, learning, teaching, or training." In Ephesians 6:4, it is used to speak of the training of a child for godly living. In Titus 2:12, the verb form was used to speak of instruction for denying ungodliness and worldly lusts in our Christian lives. In 1 Corinthians 11:32, Paul uses the word to refer to the Lord's discipline of the Christians who were receiving communion improperly. As a result, some had become sick or even died.

The word refers to God's process of training to make us holy (wholly different from the world).

In verse 8, the author continues, "But if you are without discipline, of which all have been made partakers, then are you illegitimate, and not children." True believers are always disciplined by their Father. People who claim that they are Christians but are never disciplined for their sin cannot be true children of God. Then in verse 10, the author says, "For they indeed, for a few days, punished us as seemed good to them." Earthly fathers discipline us for a few days to help us be good in this life, but God has something greater in mind. He adds, "But he for our profit, that we may be partakers of his holiness." God trains His children to partake of His own holiness. We are provided a chance through God's training process to experience what He experiences - His holiness.

In verse 11, the inspired writer asserts, "All chastening seems for the present to be not joyous, but grievous." We do not like God's discipline. It can be extremely unpleasant. Yet, the results are so powerful. He finishes, "Yet afterward it yields the peaceful fruit of righteousness to those who have been exercised thereby." The training is for righteous living which brings forth peace. In our context, it is the peace we will have in our relationships. How do the consequences of our actions fit into God's discipline? The consequences for actions are often the very discipline God uses to keep us on the right path. The consequences make us say to ourselves, "I better not do that again. That was too painful! I never ever want to experience that again!"

Consequences built into our relationships that we have to accept for sinful actions are there to train us not to do them again. When we accept the consequences and bear the brunt of what we did, it lessens the likelihood we will repeat what we did. This will then cause us to be far more righteous and experience peace in our relationships. Attempting to dodge the bad consequences, to guilt others into removing difficult consequences, or to brow beat them into rescinding painful consequences is a direct action against God, our Father, and His sanctification process instituted for our holiness.

Believers often do this because they mix up in their minds God's punishment process with His discipline training. We tend to think consequences are punishment, but believers no longer receive punishment (Romans 8:1). Christians receive the consequences of what they do to teach them to remain in the righteous path. To repeat Paul's farming analogy, if we discover that sowing good seeds reap the fruits of eternal life, this will encourage us to continue sowing good seeds. If we are sowing bad seeds and poor crops (bad consequences) are produced, this will discourage us from sowing the bad seeds. This cause and effect (sowing and reaping) will teach and train us to live righteously, especially when it entails our relationships. We must have these consequences.

As with restitution, the accepting of every consequence is a part of the repentance process and not forgiveness. People we have wronged should forgive us whether we decide to accept the consequences or not. But like restitution, it does demonstrate to them our repentance. Also, it helps to rebuild the relationship. It is not penance for sin nor is it works for our forgiveness. This is an important difference.

At times, God will use the government to intervene in our dispute. When a wrong is done to another and is against the law, whether we repent or not, there may be consequences. In Romans 13:1-4, Paul indicates that the government is the arm of God to provide consequences for grievous sins. In verse four Paul explains, "For he is a servant of God to you for good. But if you do that which is evil, be afraid, for he doesn't bear the sword in vain; for he is a servant of God, an avenger for wrath to him who does evil." To learn from their mistakes, the saints must take the punishment that the law demands. This again demonstrates their true repentance. If someone acts as if he or she has done nothing wrong and resists the law, how can this portray sorrow over his or her sin?

It is important to understand that sometimes God will not use natural consequences for sin but deal directly with His children. There are numerous examples of this in both the Old and New Testaments. Since God does not speak to us directly any longer, He may bring a trial from some kind of odd circumstances or perhaps one that seems like it came out of nowhere to get our attention. When this occurs, we should ask ourselves if we are in the midst of committing sins which the Lord God wants stopped. So, it is important to accept the consequences of sin. We learn from them.

An Ancient Portrait

A great example of the acceptance of the consequences for one's sins in a relationship is found in a parable told by our Lord in Luke 15:17-31. This is the tale of the Prodigal Son. In this story a son rebels against his father, repents, and is then restored based on the father's love and grace, not the son's works. The Pharisees saw God as accepting only those who had a righteousness from good works, rather than faith. It did not matter the evil that was in their hearts. Jesus told this tale to demonstrate that God will seek out even the outcasts of this world, call them, forgive them, and accept them into His kingdom apart from works. The heart is what matters. Though this is the key intent of this story, it also teaches other principles of forgiveness as well. One is the truths of this passage concerns accepting every consequence when one sins against another.

A certain man had two sons. The younger son demanded from his father all of his inheritance. In that culture, he was essentially saying that he wished his dad was dead, so he could cash him out. The father should have slapped him in the face, dismissed him from the family, and treated him as dead. The town would then rebuke, scorn, and shun him for such disrespectful behavior. This would have been a typical Jewish response. Instead, the father breaks with all forms of tradition and gives him one-third of all he had. This was the younger son's portion (Deuteronomy 21:17).

The father would remain in the full management of the property until his death. His son could sell his portion but the buyer would have to wait until the owner (father) died to collect. It would be a future investment for a buyer. The first born son would manage the property and then retain the rights to the remaining two-thirds which were not sold. This was the ancient custom for handling inheritances.

The son cashed out and took off to a very distant Gentile country. It was a place where he would not be known, and it would be inhabited by citizens who would not even know his traditions or customs of behavior. Also, these non-Jewish citizens would be very unfamiliar with either His God or His God's laws. This way, he was absolutely free to behave any way that he desired. He proceeded to waste all of his money. He squandered assets that had been passed down from one generation to another in his family on riotous living. He had committed all the sins that money could buy. He spent and spent while he partied and partied until it was all gone. He consumed everything until he was left with nothing.

For the first time in his life, he became virtually penniless and utterly destitute. Then a famine came, and there was no food in the land. Everyone was starving, including him. So this impoverished son decided to attach himself (Jesus uses the word "glued") to a citizen of the land. This term "citizen" would have meant that he was a man of means, and yet he did not have much interest in helping him. This is why the son ended up in the rich man's field feeding the pigs. A good Jewish boy could not eat or even touch the carcass of such an unclean animal (Deuteronomy 14:8; Leviticus 11:7). This was a fitting place to end such an epic episode of one man's rebellion. Yet, Jesus describes how he found God. It is often out of some deep desperation that we turn back to God. He truly welcomes us just as this father did with his son.

As he was feeding the pigs, he began to desire the pods that the pigs were eating. He was so hungry that this now crazed son literally fought the pigs for their left-over food. No one was available to help him get it. In the midst of this terrible condition of chaos and dying of starvation, he came to his senses. He woke up from his sinful stupor and took a hard look at his predicament. He had gotten himself into a huge mess. Then his heart changed, and the son completely repented. Obviously, he confessed his wickedness, mourned over the evil he had done, and turned from his sins; this is implied. The rebellious son decided that he ought to return home and declare to his father that he had sinned against heaven and him. He knew that he was not worthy to be his father's son; instead, he would beg to be a day-laborer.

The point of requesting to be a day-laborer indicated the son's intent to pay back the entire amount he had spent, no matter how long it took. Not only was he willing to make restitution but willing to accept the consequences of his sin, even if it meant holding the lowest position on the estate. Even the slaves had shelter and food. All he would receive was perhaps a job every day, if there was work available.

To return, this wayward son would also have to face the consequences of shame and humiliation from so many. This would include the townspeople, his father, and his older brother. He did not care. He would accept and bare it all. He would not attempt to dodge, guilt his father into removing, or brow beat him into rescinding the humiliating outcome of his foolish actions. He had to learn from his mistakes. As he approached the town, the father had been waiting for him. He ran swiftly to his son and hugged him, kissed him, and also forgave him.

Most know the rest of the story. The son was not required to do restitution or bare any of the consequences of his sin except for the starvation of the famine. This was solved by his loving father who provided a magnificent feast for him. Perhaps, if Jesus Christ was teaching on the importance of accepting the consequences of his sin, the outcome might have been quite different. Jesus is teaching the Pharisees the absolute free gift of eternal life without works, so the father had to offer all to the son because that is what God does at salvation.

We will look at the rest of this story in another part of the book. As can be clearly seen from the son's poor behavior, accepting the consequences is a part of repentance. Whether we must make the restitution or suffer the consequences is up to the person wronged, the governing authorities, or even God. Yet, we must accept every consequence that may arise.

A Modern Anecdote

One day, two male friends came into my office obviously upset with one another. They explained that normally they would not think this was a matter for counseling, but their college pastor referred them to me. He knew that they had been best friends since the first grade, and he did not want them to lose the relationship they had. Everyone watched

41

them grow up together in the church and wanted them to reconcile. After a few sessions, I discovered that they were attending college together and shared an apartment. Since Steve's parents were willing to co-sign on the apartment, it was in his name alone.

Every month, John would pay his friend Steve half of the rent and utilities in cash, and Steve would pay the bills. Then one day, John came home to see a sign posted on the front door indicating that they were being evicted. This occurred because Steve had not paid three month's rent. Of course, John blew up and started shouting at Steve. He demanded to know exactly what had happened. His roommate could not understand how Steve could not have paid the rent since his parents were supporting him, while John had to work. Steve began with a long list of pathetic excuses, but none of them were adequate to explain why the rent wasn't paid.

Finally, John gave up and went downstairs and paid the three month's rent. Six months later, the same thing occurred again. Steve had the same litany of excuses with no real reason for not paying the rent. He had now had enough and was going to move out and never speak to Steve again. It was time for a closer examination of the facts. It turns out that Steve had always been irresponsible. Since John liked Steve so much, he simply ignored it for so long that John almost became unaware of it. Steve had low grades, was always fooling around in his classes, missed his SAT's three times, couldn't hold down a decent job, and finally got into college because his dad knew someone who knew someone.

When they were younger, every time they went over to Steve's house, his parents would complain about his poor grades and lazy behavior but never did anything. He had never been disciplined, and John knew that one day Steve's nonsense would catch up to him too. What John did not anticipate (and really should have) was that Steve would be involved when it finally happened. I explained to John that it was time for Steve to accept consequences for his actions or he would never learn to take responsibility. This did not mean the drastic measure of destroying their friendship over it. It did mean that John would have to move out and find another roommate, and let Steve learn from his mistakes.

Before he did that, John thought he should give Steve one more chance, by having him put three month's rent in a savings account with John's name on it in case this were to happen again. In the Old Testament, the Lord gave Israel so many warnings and opportunities, before He judged them. As a result, John should give Steve one final chance. If it happens again, he should close the savings account, pay the back rent and move out. All of the other aspects of their relationship could remain in place; they simply could not become financially dependent on one another again.

I told him, he should sit Steve down and explain all of this to him in a very calm manner. The Lord God has set consequences into place to help define relationships and build them. Once the pressure was off John, he could finally enjoy the friendship they had as kids. It is so important that we do not constantly bail people out of their self-imposed problems because we love them. Believers should allow all people to accept the consequences of their mistakes and sins in order for them to learn from them. This is the way of the Lord. This is one of the loving methods our Father uses to discipline us as His children. This is even the way a loving human father behaves. It is the basic blueprint for the raising of human children and the raising of God's children.

A Personal Response

Dear Heavenly Father,

I recognize you are present everywhere I go and view everything I do. While I was reading this chapter, I realized that I have not fully accepted the consequences for the sins I have committed towards (add name). I am so sorry. Please help me accept the consequences and do what I am required to do in order to reconcile the relationship. Help me to honor and glorify You in my relationship with (add name) and follow your Word. I pray this in the name of Jesus. Amen.

Chapter 4

Gently Confront Sin

Once we have asked both God and the others involved for their forgiveness, it is time to consider the responsibility of the others. They may have played a part in the destruction of or break up of the relationship. If they did, then we must gently confront them. This is the last step we take when we ask others for forgiveness. It is also the first step we take when others have sinned against us.

As a result, this becomes the last step in our transgressing of others (Part 2) and the first step in others transgressing us (Part 3). This is such an important point. Even if others started the conflict and bear more responsibility, we must take ours first. Once we have owned up to what we did, no matter how great or small, then and only then, can we gently confront others for what they did. Both of these processes involve gently confronting sin. As a result, this one principle will be studied in both contexts.

A Typical Scenario

Have you ever had or heard a conversation with a spouse, parent, or friend about your neighbor that went something like this? You say or hear (holding a torn dress shirt in your hand), "I have had it with that neighbor! Every discussion we have gets ugly. There will be no more arguments about who was the greatest president ever to serve. We both got angry, I threw a soda in his face, and he ripped this shirt. I am going over there right now to give him a large piece of my mind for ruining my good clothes. (Pause for a thought.)

45

Wait! I cannot possibly behave that way. It will utterly ruin my relationship with him. He is a neighbor and a friend after all. Besides, I now realize that I bear responsibility for what happened too. I am now going to have to go over there and apologize."

In this simple illustration both parties bear responsibility for transgressing their relationship. Usually, one will begin a problem with a sinful word or action, then another responds sinfully and then they go back and forth. This destroys many relationships. Both are required to ask for forgiveness for the sins they committed. They must leave the response of the other to God. We ask and leave it up to God to prompt the other to ask also. We also depend on God for the other to graciously accept the request.

A Scriptural Principle

The next principle that must guide our reconciliation with others will address both of these common occurrences (final step and the first step) which demand a gentle confrontation. Principle four is "we must gently confront those who have sinned against us." The definition that I will use for the word "confront" in our discussion will be this: to face people and explain exactly what they did wrong. It will not include its usual negative connotation of hostility.

This is a time of mutual information exchange, not a time of bitter and angry confrontation. We explain our motives and reasons for what we did and then give them a chance to explain theirs. We may describe what we think are their transgressions, and they may add our own transgressions to the discussion. We try and discover what actually happened, not what we think occurred. This will help in the important process of clearing things up.

46

A Biblical Explanation

To gently confront sin is the final step in reconciling with those we have transgressed. It is the first step in reconciling with others who have transgressed us. Let's face it, in most conflicts we both will bear responsibility for the many evil words spoken and actions taken. We may have more or less responsibility, or an equal amount. At times, one party may have no responsibility. In any of these cases, we are required by our Lord to go and reconcile the relationship. If we have sinned in any way, we must ask for forgiveness. Once this is granted, then we should gently confront them concerning their part in the problem. If we do not feel we have sinned, then we must approach them with a gentle confrontation. This important step will also allow them to confront us, in case we are unaware of our sin.

When a transgression occurs, people usually wait for the other to approach them. Jesus does not provide this option for the people of His kingdom. Instead, in Matthew 5:23-24, Jesus proclaimed, "If therefore you are offering your gift at the altar, and there remember that your brother has anything against you, leave your gift there before the altar, and go your way. First be reconciled to your brother, and then come and offer your gift." Notice, the Lord Jesus said that if others have something against us we are to go to them, not if we have something against them. Notice also, the Lord does not say that if someone has something against us and we bear most of the responsibility for what happened, then we ought to go. He did not assign any weight of responsibility or guilt to the person who was to go. If we have any responsibility, we are to go.

On certain occasions, we may actually think that we bear no responsibility for any sin in the conflict; then, we should go to them and gently confront their sin against us. This is the first step in handling all who transgress us. In Matthew 18:15. Jesus declares, "If your brother sins against you, go, show him his fault between you and him alone. If he listens to you, you have gained back your brother." If we do not go to confront them, they may not know there is a problem.

Often times, we think that others should be able to figure out on their own what they did to us. We will say, "If they knew me, they would know what they did or if they weren't so selfish they would know what they did." This assumes that either they are able to read our minds or know what is deep inside our hearts. Only one man (God-man) could do this and that person was Jesus. They are not the Lord, so we should allow them to be human and explain to them what they did. Both of these biblical passages imply that even if we think we carry no responsibility for what happened, we must go anyway. The fact that a problem occurred between us is enough reason to approach someone to reconcile.

This confrontation has several critical purposes. First, it provides an opportunity to discuss the facts and come to an agreement as to what actually happened. Sometimes, the message we send in our words and actions are not really what we may have intended. Other times, we think we said something that may have been in our minds but was not actually spoken. Often, in the heat of the moment we think someone said or did something when they did not. We are fallible and get things mixed up. This process allows a time for figuring out exactly what was said and done.

We can discern what message was sent and how each felt about it. This provides a great opportunity to share feelings. When feelings are aroused they cannot simply be dismissed. Also, we are a product of all of our various experiences. Therefore, a word or action may mean one thing to us and a very different thing to others. These meanings produce very powerful emotions. Because they are not our feelings, we may dismiss them. This destroys relationships. Our lives, views, values, and feelings are not the only valid ones. Our partners have lives, views, values, and feelings that are also valid. These must be communicated and acknowledged by both parties, especially when they are different. This gentle confrontation process will allow this kind of communication to occur.

The second purpose is that it allows us to repent of our sins. Once the facts are clearly seen, responsibility can be taken and repentance will follow. Third, it allows others to repent of their sins. God desires this repentance. Fourth, it provides the opportunity to reconcile and "gain back" the relationship with a fellow believer. In the end of Matthew 18:15, Jesus explains the purpose, "If he listens to you, you have gained back your brother." The relationship will be rebuilt and restored. Fifth, it allows an unbeliever to repent of the sin and perhaps receive Jesus as Savior and Lord. Is not the confrontation of sin an essential part of the gospel message (Romans 1:18; 3:23)? Is it supposed to be sort of a generic sin message or can it deal with specific sins? In Acts 2:23, Peter indicted the Jews for crucifying Jesus. That is very specific. In Acts 7:52-53, Stephen spoke specifically of the transgressions of the Jewish leaders: killing the prophets, the Righteous One (Jesus), and refusing to obey God's law.

Sixth, it helps Christians escape from the snare of the Devil. In 2 Timothy 2:24-26, Paul writes, "The Lord's servant must not quarrel, but be gentle towards all, able to teach, patient, in gentleness correcting those who oppose him." Here, Timothy is encouraged to correct those who oppose him. Then, Paul explains the reason for this, "Perhaps God may give them repentance leading to a full knowledge of the truth, and they may recover themselves [come to their senses and escape] out of the devil's snare [trap], having been taken captive by him to do his will." Notice, the apostle explains to Timothy that his correction will lead to these true believers escaping the snare and trap that the Devil had them in. The Devil can capture Christians into a wrong kind of thinking which can destroy many of their relationships.

This is exactly what happened in the church at Corinth and Galatia, among others. Certain false prophets had risen up against Paul and opposed Him. Both of these examples are studied in length elsewhere in this book. Suffice it to say, the Serpent of Old was at work attempting to destroy his relationship with these saints. Seventh, it allows the church to become involved if we cannot work out the differences between us. In Matthew 18:17, the Lord Jesus describes the involvement of the church in these words, "If he refuses to listen to them, tell it to the assembly." This is an important truth to consider.

This confrontation must be done in gentleness. It is not an angry or bitter engagement. I have frequently heard people say, "We like to fight things out." This is not God's way. As Paul mentioned to Timothy, there is no quarreling; instead, there is gentleness and patience. In Galatians 6:1, the apostle describes turning a fellow Christian back from sin, "Brothers, even if a man is caught in some fault, you who are spiritual must restore such a one in a spirit of gentleness; looking to yourself so that you also aren't tempted." We must be gentle because we could fall at any time and may find ourselves in the same situation. Also, it is important to be gentle because the other person may point out a sin or sins we could have committed or a fact or assumption that we may have wrong.

There is no actual time frame or statute of limitations for this process of gentle confrontation. If someone has wronged us in the past, we can still go years later and gently confront them or ask for forgiveness to heal the wounds in our own life and theirs. As a counselor, I often suggest that my clients work out issues with parents or children even though the transgressions may have occurred years before. The wounds are still there and cannot fully be healed or the relationships reconciled without a gentle confrontation. It is God's way! What a beautiful pattern the Lord God has established for His children: repent, confront, repent and then forgive. This is God's blueprint for living and cannot be circumvented. At times, we might not want to confront unbelievers because we think they will be driven away from the good news, or believers will turn away from God. As believers, we must obey God, and let God through His Son and Spirit handle the other people's reaction.

An Ancient Portrait

The proper and improper steps of this gentle confronting of sin are illustrated through the interaction of two sisters, Martha and Mary with Jesus. This is found in Luke 10:38-42. While Jesus was out preaching the gospel, He decided to stay the night at their house. You can imagine how excited the sisters would be, but both had very different reactions. Once Martha welcomed Jesus into her home, Mary parked herself right next to Jesus and began to listen to Him teach.

Luke recorded that Mary sat at the feet of Jesus and heard His word. Sitting at a person's feet was an expression that meant to get as close as you can to hear them as they spoke. The Greek word translated "heard" means more than just hearing someone speak, but it would include "attending to, attempting to understand, and considering what is being said." In the Greek, the tense of this verb is in the imperfect active indicative demonstrating a continuous action in past time. Mary was listening as the Lord was speaking. This was the Lord of the all teaching truth, and she was learning.

51

But where was Mary's sister? Why wasn't she also sitting at the feet of our Lord Jesus? What was Martha doing? She was attempting to serve the Lord by preparing a fine meal for him. Unlike Mary, Martha was working in the kitchen. Luke described her as "distracted with much serving." The Greek word translated "serving" is the word for "ministry" in the New Testament. Martha was ministering to the Lord in a different way. Mary's sister was ministering to the Lord by handling all the preparations for His stay. What a selfless and wonderful act of kindness. Then she got "distracted" by it. The Greek word which is translated "distracted" means "dragged away with, over-occupied, too busy with." She got dragged away with the work, and it suddenly had become overwhelming. Why? Luke explains that there were "much" preparations. Perhaps, she intended to put something nice together but not too elaborate. Then she got carried away, and suddenly there seemed to be so much to do. So, the task got bigger and bigger in her mind. Allowing Mary to sit and listen to the Lord seemed fine at first, but now the entire thing became too much for one human being to handle.

Then she had really had enough. Martha was in the other room while Mary was enjoying the time with Jesus, and she was missing out! Luke writes that she "came up" to Jesus. The Greek word translated "came up" means "to come up and stand over." The Lord would have been seated in a place of honor outside in the home's courtyard (like our backyard patio). Mary would have been seated in front of Him, rather than to the side. She was listening. There most likely would have been other guests who had come to hear Jesus. In the midst of this, Martha just marches right in and would have stopped any conversation that might have been going on among the people with Jesus.

Standing over the both of them, obviously like an enraged mother whose children had made a mess, they needed to clean up; she began to let the Lord have it! She doesn't even talk to Mary but goes right to the top. She chastises the Lord for allowing Mary to get out of all the work and leave her stuck with the preparations. Martha scolds, "Lord, don't you care that my sister left me to serve alone?" Martha accuses the Lord of being insensitive to her problems and showing favoritism to her sister. This is the Master of the universe. Couldn't Jesus see how stressed, upset, and overwhelmed she was with everything? Doesn't He care about her?

Here Martha accuses her sister Mary indirectly of leaving her alone to serve Jesus. The Greek word translated "left" means "to leave or to abandon." Martha felt abandoned by her sibling Mary and completely alone. Then after accusing Jesus of such an insensitive act, her audaciousness continues. Then Martha directs, "Ask her therefore to help me." This sister of Mary basically demanded the Lord to command Mary to help her. Actually, Martha does the right thing, only in the wrong way. The woman felt wronged, and according to Matthew 18:15, what should she have done? She should have gently confronted the sins. So that part was righteous and according to biblical principles. Unfortunately, all the rest went terribly wrong.

First, a gentle confrontation implies that one is not angry. We cannot be gentle and angry at the same time. Remember our use of the word "confront." Martha was not "facing the person and dealing with the issue;" but rather, she dealt with the problem in a very argumentative and hostile manner. Second, we are to go to them privately, not in front of others or to the authority over them. Third, we're to go with the intention of restoring a relationship, not to incite more anger and destroy what we have. Martha should have come up to her sister and excused herself. Then, she should have asked to speak to Mary in private having a gentle smile of an intent which would encourage restoration. This is not how Martha had behaved, but it is how the Lord behaved in his response to her. Since she had made a public remark, here was a great learning opportunity for all from the master teacher.

Then Jesus responds with a gentle confrontation to restore the relationship with Him first, "Martha, Martha, you are anxious and troubled about so many things." He repeats her name to indicate the utter importance of what He was about to say. He does recognize how upset she is. The language Jesus utilizes indicates that Martha was not just anxious but overly concerned about this problem. Martha was not only troubled but in an uproar.

There was turbulence and great noise in her declaration. Martha's mind had become completely flooded, She had so so many thoughts that she was just acting on impulse. Ever been that way? Then Jesus calmly says, "But one thing is needed. Mary has chosen the good part, which will not be taken away from her." The Lord told her that Mary was not going to enter the kitchen. Martha's service was appreciated, but her sister's learning from the Lord was much more important. It would last into eternity.

The Lord Jesus makes a simple point: learning Bible truth is more important than Christian service. We need the truth because it lasts. The word translated "good" here means "the most excellent part, the best part." Service is great also, but it doesn't last. Both are essential, but truth comes first. What a beautiful story of a struggle to confront sin in a gentle way. This is not easy to do as Martha experienced and will require supernatural strength from the Holy Spirit. At times, we may want to confront sin in an argumentative and angry way as Martha did, even using the Bible as a weapon (as Martha wanted to use Jesus). Instead, we need to make our confrontation of sin gentle as Jesus did when He gave His response to Martha. It must also be in private.

A Modern Anecdote

One of the issues people have been dealing with in recent years has been an issue around their consumption of food. I received a phone call from a woman who claimed that her daughter was a Christian and needed help quickly. She had lost a lot of weight and was disappearing right before her eyes. Finally, she noticed that her daughter would eat and then immediately use the bathroom. One day, this mother listened through the door and heard the purging. She was frantic. The young lady came into my office looking gaunt and tired. I discovered that her older sister had criticized her from the time she could remember. It was always the same subject: her weight. She would constantly tell her she needed to lose weight. This produced so much anxiety in her life that she ate even more to relieve it.

She explained that her parents were always working, and so her older sister became her "mother." When she was about seventeen, she became very sick and lost a large amount of weight. The "plump" had finally left her. Suddenly, the boys began to notice her and were calling and texting her all the time. Even some of the girls in her school, who would never even look at her, started talking to her. She became popular and happy. Then the unexpected happened, she began to worry about her weight for the first time in her life. Once her appetite returned, she fell into her old eating habit that put the weight on in the first place: fast food. She adored it.

Rather than give up the fast food, she simply ate as much as she wanted and then went into the restroom and threw it up. She got the idea from a movie she had seen. At first it was disgusting, but she quickly got used to it. She thought this would be the best of both worlds. She could eat as much as she wanted and still remain slim. Eventually, the more she ate, the more she worried about getting fat. The more she worried about getting fat, the more she ate. Now, fast food was all that she thought about, and she was constantly tired.

This went on for quite some time. Now she was almost twenty-two, living at home, working for her favorite fast food restaurant, dating boys, and being tired. She felt stuck in this dilemma. In this situation we took a two-pronged approach. First, we would work on her self-esteem and food problems. To do this, we would begin with her sister whose criticism started this whole issue in the first place.

I told her that it was time that she let Jesus be her Lord (Master) and not herself, her sister, fast food, fatigue, or boys. She needed to begin to see herself, not as her sister or the society at large saw her, but how God saw her. Then she had to put away these old habits and put on the utterly new habits that Christ desired. It took many sessions and hard work to get her back on the road to good health and a life that glorified Jesus Christ. Her joy and sense of purpose returned.

The final task was to reconcile the relationships with her family. She called her older sister and asked to meet. When they met, she explained what had been happening to her and how God was working miraculously in her life. The next time they met, she explained what her older sister had done and its contribution to the weight problem.

The older sister sat there utterly speechless. She had been so young herself and had so much responsibility. The older sister told her that she did not even realize she had hurt her. She sobbed and told her younger sister how sorry she was. She was so glad that this was shared with her so she could repent. Then they hugged and looked forward to a closer relationship.

After this, the younger sister also gently confronted her parents who had given so much responsibility to her older sister. They had forced a young girl into being a mother far too early making her words far too important. Of course, they repented. Finally, the younger daughter was confronted for not handling the situation in a healthy, righteous, and holy way. This too was met with confession, sorrow, and repentance by the daughter. This becomes such a beautiful example of a gentle confrontation and how it can reconcile and restore relationships. After this, the young lady was able to move out and begin her future with her relationships in her family now rebuilt. What a powerful testimony of God's power and the importance of a gentle confrontation.

A Personal Response

Dear Heavenly Father,

Now I know that the gentle confrontation of sin is critical in the forgiveness process, and I have not done this. I have been sinned against by (add name) and have not confronted him (her). Give me the strength, boldness, and wisdom to do this. If I have also sinned against him (her), open my heart to be receptive to it. Please help me to restore my relationship with (add name). I want to honor and glorify you through this. I pray this in the name of Jesus. Amen.

Conclusion

As we conclude this book, I would like to leave us with some final thoughts about our God of forgiveness and what His Son did on the cross for us. First, if we understand the full extent of what was wrought for us on that cursed tree in order to forgive us, it will become so much easier to do the same thing for others. Second, if you read this entire book and realized that you do not understand salvation or have never received Christ as Lord and Savior, then I would like to provide that opportunity. Please do not skip this section; it may be the most important in your life.

From all outward appearances, humans seem "good" and attempt to live decent lives. This is man's concept of himself. This is not God's concept. The Almighty's view is that people all over the world and throughout the ages sin, sin, and sin again (Romans 3:23). This is a terrible and utterly destructive condition. Yet, they have ramifications that are far worse. These sins condemn us to everlasting divine retribution.

Though described briefly in the Old Testament, the Lord Jesus Christ clearly announced and proclaimed the future punishment to come. Contrary to popular belief, Jesus did not only speak of love, grace, and mercy, He also spoke of the coming judgment for sin. He declared that the judgment of sin would be everlasting punishment in a place He called "Hell." The Lord portrayed this place as an eternal inferno (Matthew 18:8) where there would be the weeping (from the sorrow) and gnashing of teeth (from the agony and anguish of suffering) continually into eternity (Matthew 8:12; 13:42, 50; 22:13; 24:51; 25:30; Luke 13:28).

Why must people face this horrific punishment? Though God is a God of love, grace, and mercy, He is also a God of great holiness, righteousness, and justice (Psalm 89:14,18). These attributes are just as much a part of His divine nature as His love, grace, and mercy. You have broken God's law as we all have and the penalty must be paid. This began with the first man Adam (Genesis 3:1-7). When this occurred, His love, grace, and mercy surfaced and a provision was made. Someone else would have to take man's place and pay the penalty. Someone who had never transgressed Him, who would never deserve punishment, and would fulfill all of God's Laws, would be substituted in man's place. This was the Son of God, Jesus Christ.

As the God-Man, He would pay the penalty for our sins in His death on the cross. Once done, the Lord God made only one provision for people to appropriate what His Son had done on the cross for them. This provision is receiving Jesus Christ as Savior and Lord. Though I cannot possibly share with you this good news in the confines of this book, I would love for you to consider purchasing my book entitled, *Finding The Light: The Kingdom of Heaven and How To Enter It.* It can be found for sale on Amazon.com. It is inexpensive and contains the full gospel message for your consideration. This message is so important and extensive that it cannot adequately be contained in a few pages at the end of a book.

If you are a believer, you must go out into the world and forgive as you are forgiven. These principles are to be lived and shared with others. You now have the tools to make your relationships last a lifetime. Go live them out and share them with others!

ABOUT THE AUTHOR

Dr. Donald Jones is currently a Christian Pastoral Counselor with thirty-eight years of experience in the fields of pastoral ministry, public education, and Christian counseling. He carries degrees and certificates from four major universities and from a variety of educational institutions. He has been a professor of Languages and Bible, a television commentator, and a featured speaker at a variety of events and seminars at churches, schools, and other organizations across the United States. He is a member in good standing of several secular and Christian professional organizations. Dr. Jones has been a published author since 1976. For further information view his website at www.donjonesphd.com.

www.ingramcontent.com/pod-product-compliance
Lightning Source LLC
Chambersburg PA
CBHW031527040426
42445CB00009B/429